DEAR FU...
A TIME C...
OF POEMS

TO THE PERSON WHO DIGS UP THIS BOOK IN THE YEAR 3,000

Hi there.
I don't know who you are,
Or what you look like.
You might have a huge head,
Big eyes
And spindly legs
Because people have watched too much
television.
Maybe you have a robot body
And need to be serviced regularly
By British Roboticom.
Maybe you're not human at all:
You could be one of the giant ants
That took over when we became extinct,
Or an alien that took a fancy to the planet
And cruelly wiped out the entire human race.
You're probably very brainy,
But I can do something you can't.
I can tell you all about my time.
But clever old you
Can't tell me anything.

David Orme

Edited by Vic Parker
Designed by Diane Thistlethwaite

Published by Hodder Children's Books 1997

10 9 8 7 6 5 4 3 2 1

ISBN 0340 68996 X

Printed and bound in Great Britain by Clays Ltd, St Ives plc

Hodder Children's Books
A division of Hodder Headline plc
338 Euston Road
London NW1 3BH

DEAR FUTURE . . .
A TIME CAPSULE
OF POEMS

SELECTED BY DAVID ORME

ILLUSTRATIONS BY
GEORGE HOLLINGWORTH

Hodder
Children's
Books

a division of Hodder Headline plc

Contents

Acknowledgements

All poems in this collection © individual authors.

Catching the Gorilla's Eye by Theresa Heine was first published in *Somewhere to Be* edited by Brian Moses on behalf of the World Wildlife Fund.

Unseen by Gerda Mayer was published in *Treble Poets 2* (Chatto and Windus, 1975).

The Green Man Dances by David Greygoose was first published in *Tracts* (Headland Publications).

Remote Control by Brian Moses was first published in *Rice, Pie and Moses* (Macmillan 1995).

Dragonflies by Joan Poulson was first published in *A Glass of Fresh Air* (Collins Pathways, 1996).

Milkman's Chant by Sue Cowling was first published by Scholastic Publications.

Things I'd Do If It Weren't For Mum/My Son was first published in *Parent Free Zone* edited by Brian Moses (Macmillan 1997).

Camels by Jane Duran was first published in *Breathe Now, Breathe* (Enitharmon Press, 1995).

Twenty-one Bracken Street by Phoebe Hesketh is published by kind permission of Enitharmon Press.

Dear Future . . .

FIRST OUT OF THE BOX,

LETTERS FROM OUR TIME TO YOURS:

WISH YOU COULD REPLY!

From Us To You

The first eight hundred years or so
Of this millennium were quite slow,
And nothing very much occurred.
No one had any bright ideas
For years and years and years and years,
And no "Eureka" shouts were heard.

But then the revolution came
(Industrial, not fire and flame)
And Spinning Jennies, gas and steam
Appeared, and mills and factories
Sprang up where once were fields and trees,
And so began Man's forward dream.

Combustion engines followed soon,
Man reached the skies and the moon.
Pictures appeared upon a screen.
Thanks to the microchip, computers
Now sit on laps of keen commuters,
And many wondrous things were seen.

The internet is surfed by hacks
Who can afford it. Mail by fax
And e-mail make for greater speed.
We have no cure for cancer, though.
Perhaps your scientists will know
The answer, and at last succeed.

That's just as far as we can go!
We can't envisage what you know,
What life you lead, what hopes, what fears
Are yours, but we would like to send
Thoughts that will space and time transcend:
Our love to you, across the years.

Pam Gidney

Hi!

I'm your great-
great-great-great-
Something-or-other

from the age of cars
and jetplanes and
computers.

I'm so glad you're there
looking at this. I'd hate
to think you've given up

poetry. You may however
be wondering what
a book is. So I'm putting in
a CD-Rom which shows
you me – your great-great-
great-great ancestor –

saying this poem, having the time
of my life and hoping
you're having the time of yours.

Matt Simpson

MM to MMM

Hail, hi, hello! Hope you can read me.
Your ancestor speaking. Me ancestor,
You descendants. How you doin', kids?

I send you gifts. (This bit's really hard.)
We don't know your world. Are you really really poor?
Dad says a subsistence economy because of

No fossil fuels; Mum says no, not like that at all,
But e-mail, the Post Office Tower and
Sydney Opera House. My brother says –
                    Oh, why bother with him?

All he thinks of is dinosaurs. Anyway, here's something
For Christmas, or whatever. Love from your ancestor.
(I've never been one before.) Grass seed, one bag

From Woollie's. Good stuff, grass. It really spreads.
Acorns, from the common, in case your oaks have died.
Plum-stones (for growing plums).
                    Those wingy sycamore seeds

(Dad says don't plant them if you haven't got a chain-saw).
Frogspawn. (I'm not telling Mum but frogs are OK,
The way they get to be eggs and tadpoles and that.
She thinks they won't last the trip, but I guess they will.)
If you eat them, I'll haunt you! The pebble
From the Berlin Wall my aunt gave me. That's history,
But it'd take too long to explain why. Tin
of Heinz baked beans. My favourite food. Mum's
Little dictionary. (Dad's idea.) I wanted you

continued 11

To have my trainers, marvels of modern technology,
But Dad said not on his Nelly, considering what
They'd cost him. Tin of coke, that we drink.

Last should have been today's paper, but Dad says certainly
Not, it's all a pack of lies, and will only
Depress the future. I think it's 'cos he hasn't finished

The crossword. Anyway, I'm sending you instead
A photo of my mountain bike. Really good, right?
Cheers, kids! Have a nice millennium.

PS Sorry about this, but my brother, the dinosaur one
He's too small to get it about how you
Don't exist yet, but he wants you to send him just

A postcard, please, to say what sort of ears,
And have you got antennae, having married ET
or something, he's only small, but he's dying to know.

He's sending you a bit of his blanket, in case it's cold.

U.A.Fanthorpe

Us and our families

Do you live in homes,
With families, or alone
In plastic boxes?

Things I'd do If It Weren't For Mum

Live on cola, crisps and cake.
Trade the gerbil for a snake.
Fall asleep in front of the telly.
Only wash when I'm really smelly.
Leave my clothes all scattered about.
Play loud music, SCREAM and SHOUT.
Do what I feel like with my hair.
Throw tantrums. Belch loud. Swear.
Paint my bedroom red and black.
Leave the dishes in a stack.
Find out what it's like to be me.
Let this list grow long.........Get free!

PS Take my savings in my hand.
Buy a ticket to Laserland.

Things I'd Do If It Weren't For My Son

Drink my morning tea in peace and quiet.
Practise yoga. Go on a diet.
Paint his room in almond white.
Dismantle the strobe light.
Give the gerbil cage away.
Keep the telly off all day.
Get the kitchen nice and clean.
Take a break from the washing machine.
Stack the CDs back on the shelf.
Have the house completely to myself.
When it's tea-time, not bother to cook.
Phone for a pizza and read my book.

PS *Go for a walking holiday in the hills.*
No *theme parks, laser quests or mega thrills.*

Tony Mitton

The Hole

Dad says it's due
      to all the aerosols we've used
      all the refrigerators in the world
      all the car belched fumes
deforestation
irradiation
luminous wristwatches
bleach
the rinse of acid rain

But I think the hole
in his hairstyle
has more to do with
growing old

Dave Reeves

16

Troublin' Hair

Lawd, if you had 'good' hair
'stead of nappy pon yuh head.
we would be saved the despair
of raking through dis dread.

Mi is tempted to leave it wiry
But mi have a sense of shame.
Mi will plait every lock
No matter how much it pain.

White folk think we dirty
That we no know soap and water
Me no care to wash away the Black.
But mi will put your hair in order.

Don't cry chile, stop weeping.
Mi is almost through.
Stand, look now in the glass
And see how beautiful is yuh.

SuAndi

Just An Ordinary Weekend

Saturday is
>
> when I stay in bed till nine
> just to prove there's no school,
> when breakfast is anything
> I can smuggle back up there.

. . . is
>
> lying in top of the duvet
> headphones tuned on
> to the latest CD
> or watching cartoons.

. . . is
>
> dad in his tattiest jeans
> laying new patio slabs
> and Tottie, our tortoise,
> lumbering off with a blob
> of cement on her back.

. . . is
>
> mum cracking jokes with
> the milkman over the bill
> then playing 'hide and seek'
> with me, needing a trolley slave
> for the shopping safari
> (she never wins!)

. . . is   deep-pan pizzas or 'quickie'
              fish and chip treats
              when she gets in,
              an afternoon of footie
              or me and the gang
              taking our bikes for a spin.

Sunday is
              when even the noises are quiet,
              cars are coralled on the drives,
              washed, spruced up,
              and mowers hum softly,
              barbering scruffy lawns.

. . . is   dad and Al from next door
              jogging off down the street,
              mum muttering "Men!",
              watching him flop exhausted
              onto the sunbed and stay there
              for two hours.

. . . is   clockwork routine.
              Mrs Brenton off to the post
              with her Lhasa Apsos,
              their cheeky bottoms and
              curtain of tails swishing
              like miniature car washes.

continued

... is   Me saying "I'm bored"
and mum saying "Here
dig the garden, then!"
Me saying "I've just remembered . . .
Sor-ry!"

... is   time for tea and talk,
an evening zapping aliens
on the computer or
just lying on the bed
thinking mega thoughts

... until   mum calls up the stairs
"Have you done your homework yet?"
and the weekend
ends.

Patricia Leighton

In Case The Fire Goes Out

Each morning Mother lit the fire;
knelt in that first anxious hour
as wavering flames cautiously explored
gaps in the cross-hatched sticks; transparent
new-born tongues that almost disappeared
when touched by winter light.
She coaxed them – placed within reach small lumps
of coal, adjusted the flow of air –
as they strengthened, moved to other rooms
but often called, "Is the fire alright?"
At frequent intervals she came again
to watch, to prod and feed
or fill the scuttle with more fuel.

Before we left the house the fire was banked
with layers of slack 'to keep it in'.
She'd wait for a conversation's lull,
gather her coat, explain: "We must get back
in case the fire goes out." Sometimes, on our return
the embers were dark as death. Then, courageously
("I'm terrified of fire," she often said)
she'd stretch large sheets of paper, close
the gaping mouth, conjure a roar of life –
amazing resurrection. By dusk the fire
throbbed heat, could tackle a hefty log, glowed
from a heart of candescent caves. Evening
after evening we gathered round that hearth.

Margaret Banthorpe

Carnival Breakfast

Mum 'n' Dad
Both in the kitchen
Doin' the breakfast
It's gonna be kickin'

Dad's makin' dumplin
Mum's fryin' plantain
Breadfruit in the oven
Green Banana's boilin'

Onions 'n' peppers
Hot oil in the pan
Saltfish added . . . plus
Ackee out the can

Hardo bread
'N' pineapple punch
This is my breakfast
This ain't my lunch

The smells are jus' wicked
It's too hard to describe it
They're torturin' my nose
I jus' wanna eat it

Carnival breakfast
Spread on the table
Get ready, set, go
I'm chillin 'n' able

Jus' about to cram
The food on my plate
Pile it up high
Then mum says "Wait"

"Go and wash your hands
Before you pick up food"
Dad jus' kissed his teeth
He's in a bad mood.

Came back from the bathroom
Looked at my plate
Dumplin, Ackee 'n' Saltfish
Jus' couldn't wait

I was happy, feelin' good
As I sat in the chair
Then I heard my Dad slappin'
His food in my ear

continued

Slap, slap, slap
All he did was smile
This went on for ages
For the longest while

Slurp slurp slurp
He went with his tea
It was drivin' me mad
It was gettin' to me

To make matters worse
Mum started too
I needed a plan
What could I do?

I slapped 'n' I slapped
I slurped 'n' I slurped
'N' then came the moment
When all of us burped

If you can't beat 'em
Join 'em . . .

Martin Glynn

A Family Meal

"Put it on," the table said.
Mother, when I brought the bread,
Tasted good. Dad licked. His lips,
Both of them, liked fish. And chip
Wash up. "Please do it now," asked Mother,
Looking at me, "And rob my brother."
Dad stretched the budgie, chattered on,
"How sad to think." Those times are gone.

Wendy Cope

Clothesline

Flap! Flap! Flap!
Clothes cracking on the line
wind-filled, billowing,
whiff of leaf
corn-sheaf
honey-sweet woodbine.

SNAP! SNAP! SNAP!
Mum catches them in turn,
smoothing, folding them –
jumpers, sheets,
teeshirts, jeans
scented basketful.

Dream ... dream ... dream ...
Dad tucks me up in bed,
fragrant wisps of outdoor things
meadows, trees,
mountains, fields
shimmer in my head ...

Una Leavy

Remote Control

When first we had a remote control for our TV,
Dad always used to sit on it so the screen went blank
or kept changing channels as he shifted his weight.
Our dog used to carry it off to his basket
then growl when anyone stooped to ask for it back.
Mum tidied it away, somewhere different each day,
while little brother made it a never-to-be-without part
of the mammoth Lego space station that
                                        consumed his room.
Grans and Grandads failed to spot it,
Knocked it off or sent it spinning.
Our neighbour's baby tried to wash it
and burglars too, once tried to flog it!

But now we're into overload, we sit and shuffle
remote controls, the stereo and the video,
satellite channels too, and something Dad brought home
called DAT which he used for a bit and then said,
                                        "That's that,
can't make head or tail of this!"
But when Mum sits down to watch TV, aims the controls
and hears instead a succession of
                                blimps and beeps and blips,
she closes her eyes and sinks back in despair.
All these gadgets just serve to confuse
when you can't even change to Channel Three for
                                        'The News'.

Brian Moses

When I'm Seventeen

When I'm seventeen I'm going to grab me a banger
all dent, buckle and clattery tin –
jack-in-the-box suspension, knocked out windows,
tyres like ship's fenders fore and aft.
I'll get her up like an earthquake in a paintshop
(except for NEXT STOP HELL and DAVE AND VICKY [in white])
and shove in a fantastic supercharger –
nicked from a spare set of aero engine plans.
And I'll enter that smasher for every event
on every track under the roaring sun.
They'll be hoarse bawling my number on the mike
as I rev fit to murder down the straight –
dance the pedals, flip the wheel,
clip the tail of the leaders slewing on the bend.
Oh I'll squeeze 'em out, shunt and crunch 'em
and if they bash me off I'll slash screaming back
and if I come off the banking daft side up
I'll be out sharp and hungry as a weasel,
sticking my helmet on a post sniffing oil and dust
till they tractor me off and throw me a spanner
to tighten her up and start again.
And I'll bellow past the chequered flag
tall as a ship's siren, loop the pack
then sit on top with the Banger Queen
doing my Lap of Honour, waving to the crowd.
And Vicky will come through the blue smoke
in her green top and hair tied back.
And when I sleep at night the bed will be spinning,
cutting corners on two wheels.

Geoffrey Holloway

Where we live

THIS IS WHERE WE LIVE.

"HOW PRIMITIVE," YOU WILL SAY.

WE LIKE IT LIKE THIS!

If I Lived

If I lived in a terraced house, traffic
would shake me.

If I lived in a castle keep, the wind
would wake me.

If I lived in a bungalow, I'd sleep
downstairs.

If I lived in a tower block, I'd fly high
in the air.

If I lived in a boat, I'd float
on slow green water.

If I lived in a caravan, I'd be
the traveller's daughter.

Gillian Clarke

Milkman's Chant

Two, four, six, eight,
Crash the bottles in the crate!
Six, eight, two, four,
Daily service to your door.
Four, six, eight, two,
Red top, silver top or blue?
Eight, two, four, six,
Don't forget the spondulix
For the M.I.L.K.O. – Milko!

Sue Cowling

Leisure Centre

Do you know
what a Leisure Centre is ?

Lots of people think
it's one of those places
where you go to work out in the gym,
to play badminton or squash,
maybe to swim,
or to bounce your flab on a trampoline.

Wrong.
That is not a Leisure Centre.

In my sitting room at home,
there's a soft sofa,
with a low table next to it
where I put my can of beer,
my crisps,
my chocolates
and my TV control.

That's a Leisure Centre.

Mike Jubb

Dark Day

Lamposts stand like sparklers
spitting rays of light into the night

blobs of yellow jellyfish
wriggle in pathway puddles.

Bullets of rain riquochet,
run rivers in sleeve creases,

make lakes across boxed lunches
of crushed crisps, sandwiches

clutched by huddled children
on a dark day way to school.

Gina Douthwaite

Latchkey Cats

I live on a long terrace
where cats sit out on doorsteps,
watching passers-by.
Not always the same cat
at the same front gate.

I think that lots of cats
live in two homes – two owners
forking sticky catfood,
pouring milk; two shifts
of owners for each cat,
each daily programme.

Household One off to work,
cat out and front door closed.
The morning gateside watch.
Along to Household Two,
lunch and a quiet bask
in doorstep sunshine.
Indoor for teatime; then
a miau to be let out and stroll
away to wait by front door One,
offer homecoming welcome
(purr, rub against legs, etc).
Supper. Sleep.
Each answers to two names,
those lazy latchkey cats,
living their double lives,
eating their double meals
and getting fat.

Pamela Gillilan

The Village Shop

Push the door. Ssh! Don't tell.
Listen to the old shop bell.
Imagine what they used to sell
Fifty years ago –

Gobstoppers and Cherry-lips,
Humbugs, Sherbet, Lemon Pips
in little pointed paper slips.

Home from school, to the shop,
Beano, butter, lemon pop,
papers, stamps, ring-ring, non-stop
Yesterday.

Flip-flops, knickers, Pogs and wellies,
String and bottle gas and jelly,
Sugar, carrots, vermicilli.

Now we drive to the supermarket.
Fumes and traffic. Stop and park it.
Fill the trolley. Pay by credit.

No more running down the street
when we run out of milk. No treats.
No kind hand with extra sweets.

No shop. No school. No bus. No train.
No quiet little country lanes.
Just fumes and ozone in the air
and hurry, hurry everywhere.

Gillian Clarke

The Precinct Pack

They're the precinct posers
Strutting the slabs.
Saturday freedom,
Weekend up for grabs.

Kenny's got the latest jeans,
Josie's slick in silk,
Dan's best leather
Yells A C E in gilt.

Ann fancies Stuart,
Whispers it to Lou,
Lou tells Trevor,
Trevor tells Stu.

Lolling on the benches,
Propping up the bins,
Laughing faces
Split with grins.

They're the precinct peacocks.
Really got the knack
Of making all the others
Wish they were in the pack!

Patricia Leighton

Shopping Jungle

Through the spinning entrance
into a bright, buzzing jungle
where we hear the clank and swish
of trollies that are laden, yet still
ambitious for more exotic cargo.

High in the unseen canopy
a nearly familiar music
drips onto banks of bananas,
pink grapefruit, clementines,
and ranks of packaged vegetables.

Then, lost among spices, yogurt,
sauces, we find a crosspath that leads
to another harvest of firelighters,
soap, cereal, cheese, and an oasis
of exquisite still or fizzy water.

The jungle ends at the checkout
where item by compulsive item
is counted and charged before we
can wheel out the fruits and follies
through the gateway of Ostec jungle.

John Fairfax

Mr Khan's Shop

is dark and beautiful.
There are parathas,

garam masala,
nan breads full of fruit.

There are bhajees, samosas, dhal,
garlic, ground cumin seeds.

Shiny emerald chillies
lie like incendiary bombs.

There are bhindi in sacks,
aaloo to eat with hot puris

and mango pickle. There's
rice, yoghurt,

cucumber and mint –
raitha to cool the tongue.

Sometimes you see
where the shop darkens

Mr Khan, his wife
and their children

round the table.
The smells have come alive.

He serves me
puppadums, smiles,

re-enters the dark.
Perhaps one day

he'll ask me to dine with them:
bhajees, samosas, pakoras,

coriander, dhall.
I'll give him this poem: *Sit down*

young man, he'll say
and eat your words.

Fred Sedgwick

City Sounds Heard After Dark

The sweesh sweesh of speeding cars.
Old songs from the crowded bars.
Disco drums and loud guitars.

Aircraft zapping through the sky.
Rooftop cats that spit and cry.
Laughter from the passers-by.

Motorbikers' sudden roar.
Corner lads who josh and jaw.
A call. A shout. A slammed door.

The guard dogs that howl and bark.
Voices from the padlocked park.
City sounds heard after dark.

Wes Magee

School

SCHOOL IS WHERE WE LEARN.
WE DON'T PLUG CHIPS INTO OUR
BRAINS; WE NEED TEACHERS!

What Teachers Dream

Teachers dream of 4 o'clock
and coffee lightly stirred,
they dream of quiet children
who hardly say a word.

They dream of summer holidays
and chairs which never scrape,
they dream of no wet playtimes
and children never late.

They dream of banning bubble gum
they dream of playing pool
but, mostly, teachers dream
of there being no more school.

Andrew Collett

Winter Break

Katie's lucky.
She's been told
to stay inside at break.
I wish I had a cold!

Ahmed's lucky.
He got only two
on Monday's spelling test.
I wish I had to stay inside
to learn the rest!

Our teacher's lucky.
Each break-time Mr. Mould
drinks coffee in the staffroom.
I wish I was old!

Each day's the same.
The sky is grey,
the wind is cold
but *still* they say,
"Off you go now,
out to play!"

It's never *me* who's told
to stay inside.
I hate it,
yes, I *hate* it,
stuck out here in the cold!

Judith Nicholls

Take Note

I wrote her a note
saying
SEE YOU AT THE DISCO AT 7
I passed it back
to John,
said
"Pass it on,"
he passed it back
to Jack,
said "Pass it on"
to Yvonne . . .

Yvonne opened it.
It crackled.

Mrs Perry looked up,
we all looked down
then I turned round.

Yvonne was smiling,
she'd gone red.

"Pass it back,
pass it back!"
I said.

Her smile fell off her face.
"Pass it back"
I said,

"to Laura."
Yvonne smiled,
then tore a
strip and a strip
tore the whole thing into bits
threw it up into the air
and I could only sit and stare.

She pointed to her lips,
whispered
"See you at the disco"

And I turned round
and banged my head on the desk
and banged my head on the desk
and banged my head on the desk

with a loud, slow sound.

Ian McMillan

Mr Venables and the Winnie The Pooh Watch

Part I – The Beginning of Games

When Mr Venables bellows,
"Valuables!"
Treasures are surrendered,
Placed in two plastic boxes;
One marked 'Jewellery',
The other marked 'Watches'.

Part II – The End of Games

When Mr Venables bellows
"Valuables!"
Hands dive,
Fingers peck,
Retrieve adornments for
wrist and neck.

Mr Venables examines his two containers
And pulls out a watch, "Any claimers?"

There must be someone who
Will admit to owning this 'Winnie The Pooh'.
No one responds by raising a hand,
To claim the watch with the furry wristband.

Part III – The 'End of School' Bell is Thirteen Seconds Late

Mr Venables checks with the watch on his wrist;
The Winnie The Pooh, that nobody missed.

John Coldwell

It Always Rains On Sports Day

It always rains on Sports Day,
or it has for weeks previously,
and we're sitting there on coats
while the grass is steaming.
They might do better to issue us
with floats, to cope with the dozens of puddles
that punctuate our running track.
And the winner might just as well swim home,
where his winner's rosette will be pinned
to a soggy vest.

It's always fun on Sports Day,
seeing who gets wettest.
You can bet your life
it won't be the teachers,
they come prepared and swan around
beneath their golf umbrellas,
while everyone else is perched on chairs
sinking deeper into the mud.

I hate Sports Day at our school:
you're out there trying to look cool
in front of parents, brothers, sisters,
grans, grandads, aunts, uncles, cousins,
the lady from two doors down
and your girlfriend from 3C.

And then you slam down in the mud
and you look like a player
in some rugby squad
rather than the bronzed, heroic Greek athlete
that you wanted them to see.

It always rains on Sports Day,
or it has for weeks previously.

This year it rained so much
that Sports Day was cancelled.

What a shame!

Brian Moses

Exams

Exams aren't fun.
You don't get many people
going to exams for their holidays.

They don't show exam highlights
on Match of the Day,
there's no Exam of the Month competition
or action replays.

You can't chew or drink exams
and when you put them on
they're really dull and dated.

No, exams aren't cheerful.
Imagine taking an exam to the disco,
who'd do that?

Or paying to see one dance and sing
at an end-of-the-pier show?

You'd think my teachers
would agree with me, see
the reason in what I'm saying.

If exams had been here years ago
they'd all have been hanged
for sleep stealing.

David Harmer

School

When I think of school I remember
Standing in the corner
Looking at the wall
Standing in the corridor
Doing nothing at all
Standing outside the Head's room
Will I get the strap?
Standing on a chair in gym
For answering teacher back.

When I think of school
I can't remember much
About English, History or French.
But I can remember my lines
Hundreds and thousands of them.

I will not do this
I will not do that
I will pay attention
I will not talk back
I will not eat chocolate or toffee or sweets
I will pay attention and not snore whilst asleep.

School had a party on my leaving day
The teachers seemed happy that I was going away.
I regret now I'm older that I never understood
That in order to be educated
The first rule is to be very very good.

SuAndi

Camels

for Syra

On your first day of secondary school
we set off in a minicab.
I know you've been awake since dawn,
preparing, worrying in your room
blue and draped as a tent.
Your braids are tightly knit.
Hands in your lap.
The small red and white checks
of your collar stick out
over your grey wool coat
like the slightest mention
of candlelight in a village
before morning, that first voice.

The driver is Moroccan, lifts out
Andalus from the loudspeaker
to remind us of the shimmering world
beyond the school, its breathlessness
and turquoise particles never ceasing,
the camels with their wide-of-the-mark
and fluid sidestepping, blinking
with their great neutral eyelids
sand-light, night,
their own lives whirling within them
far from our own, on the way
to school in a minicab.

continued

The school is still far,
floating over Regent's Park.
You take out your new pencil case
with nothing missing.
We trail the Andalus song
like a slow scarf, like a beach-tide
across the windows of the car.
We can see over the gates of the school.
The other children arrive –
they are all courageous.
You take the measure of them
when their camels drop to their knees
and they slide down the rugs,
the four corners slipping.

The older girls wait
at the top of the steps,
bend down tenderly,
ask your name.

Jane Duran

Our wide world

IT'S A LOVELY WORLD.

WE HOPE WE WON'T HAVE WRECKED IT

BEFORE YOU GET IT.

The Stuck-on-the-A1 Party

On a sunny afternoon near Barnsley
we're side by side by side
by side by side
in the biggest traffic jam
since I don't know when,
and the guy in the car next door
leans out and shouts,
"Let's have a stuck-on-the-A1 Party!"

So we fetch the picnic baskets
and the bottles of pop.
We get really friendly
and play silly games,
like "Guess when the traffic
will start up again!"

We play 'Postman's Knock'
and this huge french lorry driver kisses Mum
and looks as if he'd like to do it again
till Dad says, "Watch it chum!"

And a guy in a van selling novelty goods
hands out party hats, balloons
and those things that you blow
to make a rude noise.

And caterers, off to some wedding,
pass round the vol-au-vents and the chicken drumsticks.
"We'll never make it now," they say.
We swap addresses with people

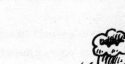

from the car in front,
"If you're ever up this way again,
look us up . . ."

And then when a shout comes
to say that we're moving on,
everyone says what a great time they've had,
and couldn't we do it again sometime?

And I'm thinking that maybe they'll really catch on,
these A1 parties – they're really fun!

Brian Moses

continued

Carnival Song

Hoisted higher than us all
On your daddy's shoulders, girl.

Here is a world to see,
Here is your community.

Look out, look down,
Cry big love, spread it around.

Make it so we laugh with you,
Make old sadness pack and go.

This is everybody's street,
These are tomorrow's dancing feet.

All the colours, every skin,
A whole new life to be dressed in.

On your daddy's shoulders, girl, ride high,
Apple of our future's eye.

John Mole

The Hedgehog Warns Her Children

Beware, my children, those hard shelled monsters
With the soft masters within,
For they will crush us if we cross their paths,
With their four huge round feet.

Sometimes they purr, puffing dark clouds behind,
Sometimes they roar,
Raking the sky with sharp rods of sound;
But always they are savage
Always they are wild,
And, each one of us, they would kill.

So, my children, beware the hard shelled monsters
With the soft masters within,
Beware the monsters called . . .

                              CAR.

David R Morgan

Twenty-one Bracken Street

From Bracken Street in Bolton
You can see the moors
Stretched out like mastiffs, tawny and brindled,
Sleeping under the sun.

When I get to the dentist's
Which is Number Twenty-one,
I wish I were there
Flying my kite
Instead of clenched up in this chair,
Scared as a rabbit facing a gun.

The man in white smiles at my fear,
picks up a scalpel, scraping away.
And prods with his pick for signs of decay.
Whizz comes the drill with his "Mouth open wide" –
I shut my eyes tight,
My knuckles are white
As I feel in my pocket for something to crush,
But the drill has gone furry –
It's only a brush!

Out in the street the lion-eyed sun
Glares down as I run
Back home for my kite, but never again
Will I shake like a rabbit facing a gun
As I face the door of frosted glass
At Number Twenty-one.

Phoebe Hesketh

Catching the Gorilla's Eye

However far along
The glass frontage you slide,
He will not look at you,
But strokes back the hair
From a puzzled forehead,
Gazes beyond the faces
Peering and grimacing,
And feels in the distance
Such an intensity
Of green heat, such a
Cacophony of parrots,
That he must shade his eyes.

Theresa Heine

Dragonflies

They used to fly
over all the ponds
in summer, granny says –

like sparkling sapphire helicopters,
purple aeroplanes,
with eyes of bright topaz,
wings flashing emerald light,
brightening the countryside
in their jewelled flight.

Sun-glow brilliance winging
over every pond,
someday I hope to see one
– smallest last dragon.

Joan Poulson

Don't

Don't smoke cigarettes – don't begin!
or sunbathe – tan's cancerous to skin,

eat butter – it clogs up the arteries,
take ecstasy tablets at parties,

walk fells which are covered in bracken –
it's carcinogenic, they reckon.

Don't use mobile 'phones, excess chatter
can grow into growths in grey matter,

drink coffee for caffeine's alarming –
frays nerves when they're in need of calming

or swallow the sea for it's brimming
with sewage, so zip lips when swimming

and DON'T breathe the air – it's polluted!
with fumes to which lungs are not suited.

Don't think anyone will survive
to see the **Millennium** arrive.

Gina Douthwaite

Going Fishing

Mum can't believe I'll keep still.
"Regular fidget, you," she says.
But Dad and I, we understand.
"She'll be all right. Bring you something for tea."
"A mucky old welly, a pram perhaps."
Mum really doesn't understand.

A half-hour drive. It's barely light.
It's wonderful when no one's about –
we meet the milkman on his round,
the paper boy rubbing his eyes
perhaps, but no one else. Just us.
Everyone else is snug in bed:
well, more fool them, I think. I wouldn't
miss this for all the world.
"All right?" Dad asks. I nod. "You bet."

We've got our pitch, laid out the gear –
the rods, the bait, umbrella, net,
two canvas chairs and a crammed hamper:
to be fair, Mum's good about that,
plenty to eat and keep us warm.
At this hour, when the river's still,
it's like living in a different time

or place. The mist slowly lifts,
the sun is pushing its weak fingers
through as it starts to warm the day.
Peaceful. "Yeh, worth its weight in gold.
Now how about a cup of tea
to warm us up before we start?"

And so we sit and plan the day,
watching the currents and the play
of light and ripples, possible fish.
"Trevor says there's a monster here,
twenty or thirty pounds he says.
Maybe we'll catch him. Wouldn't Mum
be pleased?" I nod. I think she'd be
surprised how quiet I can be.

The sun warms as we choose our bait.
Will we be lucky ? We'll just wait
and see. The day stretches before us.
I'd rather be here than anywhere.

Jill Townsend

August Outing

The August Bank Holiday's here again,
With buckets and spades and pouring rain;
Bumper to bumper, we haven't got far
Before Maisie is sick in the back of the car;
The baby starts howling, Jim's pinched the last jelly
And Karen remembers that "film on the telly"
which she's wanted to look at "for weeks and weeks";
Dad loses his temper. Nobody speaks.

After 'single line traffic' and several 'diversions'
We find ourselves trapped behind coach trip excursions,
Five frozen food lorries and, I swear it's a fact, a-
head of us all is a slow-moving tractor,
Though there's no farm for miles. (Each year it's the same,
The tractor is waiting to play out its game.)

Mum's made us a picnic, with boiled eggs and ham,
Which we eat in the car in the long traffic jam.
There's a lull in the drizzle and what do we see
But a space in a layby to brew up some tea;
Then, just as our dad's got the primus stove going,
The sky turns quite black and I swear it starts snowing –
Well, sleeting at least. From the stove there's no glow,
And dad's hopping mad, dripping wet, head to toe.

Back in the car, he sits drying his hair.
"We'll make do without tea until we get there!"
Mum says, "Let's go home", but now dad's
                                    teeth are showing:
"You wanted the seaside and that's where we're going!"
When we get to the sea, there's a mist swirling round,
The car parks are full with no space to be found.
We stop in the High Street; mum puts up her brolly;
We rush to a kiosk and buy an ice lolly.
The sea-front's deserted; the cafés are full;
The amusement arcade isn't much fun at all.
We return to the car and the 'No Parking' sign
And, left by their warden, our ticketed fine.

The journey back home is as slow as a snail,
Bumper to bumper and blowing a gale.
The tractor returns and it drives dad insane
(And Maisie is sick in the back seat again).
We arrive home at last; but there's one thing that's clear –
We're sure to repeat the same nightmare next year!

(Well, I mean – Bank Holiday Monday by the sea; it's
tradition, isn't it?)

Trevor Harvey

The Green Man Dances

The Green Man dances in the wood
By withered nettles where the oaks once stood
The Green Man dances in the wood
But the trees scream murder
As we burn them down

The Green Man has danced out under the stars
Under changing skies for a million years
Silver in the morning and the coal black night
Waking again for the last long fight

The Green Man dances in the wood
By broken glass where the tall cedar stood
The Green dances in the wood
But the trees wail murder
As we axe them down

Now the Green Man grieves by the poisoned stream
Weeping bitter scalding tears
The badger, the otter and the hare lie dead
Dark rooks drift in circles as the sky turns red

The Green Man dances in the wood
By barbed wire fences where the elm once stood
The Green Man dances in the wood
But the trees weep murder
As we hack them down

continued

The Green Man danced wherever he chose
Before forests were stolen and fields enclosed
The Green Man danced before winding lanes
Twisted into the madness of motorways

The Green Man dances in the wood
By dark choking shadows where the larches stood
The Green Man dances in the wood
But the trees whisper murder
As we rip them down

The hounds bay blindly where foxes used to run
But hunt for the Green Man goes on and on
The ring of shrinking woodland tightens in a snare
As the Green Man tracks frantic as a frightened hare

The Green Man dances in the wood
By brackish water where the broad beech stood
The Green Man dances in the wood
But the trees breathe murder

As we smash them down
We'll catch him and beat him
And twist a jagged wreath
We'll whip him and scourge him
And nail him like a thief
To the highest branch
Of his last oak tree
With blackbird, dunnock, jackdaw and crow . . .
But when the Green Man dies,
We all die too.

David Greygoose

Betty Greenwood

Because she saw Earth going bald
and feared it might feel cold
without its trees,
did Betty Greenwood, as a child,
plant acorns, conkers, cherrystones,
to make a green fur-coat to warm Earth's bones.

When she grew up she bought a field
and set, till it was filled,
the sapling trees
she'd nurtured since a child:
oaks, ashes, limetrees, birch,
wild cherrytrees and chestnuts, some of each.

Years passed, and Betty Greenwood's ground
uttered the soughing sounds
wind makes in trees;
and branch to branch reached twiggy hands
to bond in lofty brotherhood
under the name of Betty Greenwood's Wood.

In Winter, branch-combed sun could pierce
the windows of her forest house
that drowned in trees
in Summer when mysterious
green rooms of her extended home
hid bird-choirs high in airy-storeyed dome.

One day old Betty locked her door
and over deep-pile forest floor,
mossed green as trees,
she walked a vaulted corridor
that led her round an endless maze
till in a glade, and meeting her calm gaze

With topaz eyes, Lord Wolf, alone,
stood waiting still as stone.
"Bess of the Trees,"
he said, "your work is done."
She stroked his head, then down a dappled track
they strolled together and did not look back.

Anna Adams

Captivating Creature

Elephant roaming in forest, on grassland,
using her trunk like a hand and an arm,
sucking up water to spray as a shower,
wafting palm ears when the sun gets too warm,
dusting herself with a trunkful of dry sand,
ripples of wrinkles encompassing eyes.
On thick pillar legs she's at peace with her power,
at ease with a brain hardly mammoth in size.

Captive Creature

Elephant restless in circus, in zoo,
pacing and pawing at concrete and bar,
longing for freedom and wide-open-spaces,
leading processions, bedecked with howdah,
drooping with feathers and wearing a tutu,
learning, on two legs, to balance and dance.
Juggling with balls. Being put through such paces
doesn't give dignity much of a chance.

Gina Douthwaite

The Road Through The Air

It's all very well for you in the future,
you can think yourselves where you want to be.
You can ponder your way to Beijing or Bombay
just by a little telepathy.

You can cross an ocean with the right notion
or go on a stroll round a mental block,
and sometimes, it seems, you have such vivid dreams
you wake up on Uranus, which must be a shock.

But for us in our present (the past, to you),
your present (our future) hasn't occurred.
Cars, trains or planes, and not fast, long-haul brains,
are the methods of transport mostly preferred.

If we're going long-distance, the road we take
is the only one that goes everywhere,
passing over the tops of lights, jams, cones and cops,
that highest of highways, the road though the air.

We get packed into a sort of long tin,
where they ply us with cushions and headphones and say
"If we crash-land, then, please, put your head on your knees.
Lifejacket . . . Oxygen . . . Have a nice day."

Then the world falls away and we're part of the sky.
The stewardess serves ice-cubes and peanuts and smiles,
and down below all of the trees have gone small,
and the queue for the loo stretches hundreds of miles.

continued

Our dinner is served in a small plastic tray.
That wedge-shape is melon, that triangle's cheese.
While we're trying to eat something vaguely like meat,
the fruit salad escapes and get mixed with the peas.

There's a film going on, but the sound track has gone,
so we can't tell what's what or remember who's who.
All that waving of arms soon loses its charms,
so we look out the window at masses of blue.

It's the sea! We had no idea how much there was
or how little it does. It just waves as we go
with its island and boats, then a cloud-field floats
in between, and we're sailing an ocean of snow.

Then they pull down the blinds and pretend that it's night,
but there aren't any beds, so we have to make do
with our seats. We're unwashed and our teeth are unbrushed,
and it's still not worth joining the queue for the loo.

There's a sort of a night, but it doesn't feel right,
then they wake us with breakfast and we're nearly there.
This time when we look down, what mountains, what town,
what forest will we see from our road in the air?

It's just not the same for you in the future,
you arrive when your journey has hardly begun.
You miss all the queues, the discomfort, the views,
and I'm sorry to tell you, you miss half the fun.

Matthew Francis

Beyond My House

Above my house
is the blue of the sky,
fragile fishbone clouds
and the wind whispering
     like an untold wish.

Below my house
is the dark secret earth,
deep-spiralling roots
and the mystery of lives
        lived underground.

Around my house
is the garden wall, where
slow snails crawl and spiders
hang their webs, beaded
        like door curtains.

Beside my house
is an apple tree, a
shady place to hide
in summer, in winter
        a bony skeleton.

continued

Over my house
is a rainbow, a magic
paint-splashed bridge
where raindrops shine
       like crystal beads.

Inside my house
is my family, my laughing,
crying, quarrelling family,
a place where I belong
       every single day.

Beyond my house
is the future, full of promise
as an unopened parcel
wrapped in fancy paper
       and silver ribbons.

Moira Andrew

Goodbye millennium

A MILLENNIUM,
A THOUSAND YEARS, HAVE GONE BY.
HERE'S TO THE NEXT ONE!

Memories

"When I was a lad,"
Said Grandad,
"We used to play in the street.
No playing with daft computers,
But kicking a ball with bare feet."

"Aye! When I was a lass,"
Said Grandma,
"My Father worked down the pit.
And all my Mother could do for fun
Was sit and knit and knit."

Now I'm just a lad
And I hold my tongue
As they talk
Of olden days.

Their memories
Of being young
Are hung in a golden
Or a dusty haze.

I don't want to argue.
I don't want to row.
I just know that I'm glad
To be living right now!

John Kitching

The Best of the Twentieth Century

If I could fill that millennium box full of splendid things,
there are many wonderful inventions
I know I'd like to bring –
the sensible, the silly, the important and the trivial –
things which have made life easier
and often more convivial.
So this is a part of an inventory
of things from the twentieth century.
Powered flight, electric lights,
Motor bikes, nylon tights, women's rights,
chocolate bars, motor cars, spaceships orbiting the stars,
instant coffee, dessert bonhoffee, mint flavoured toffee.
Oven-ready hens, ball point pens,
cures for this disease and that,
treatment for sick dogs and cats,
wide cinemascope, the Hubble telescope,
many healing drugs, non-slip rugs, silly ugli-mugs,
snug double-glazing, living-gas fires blazing,
home computers, internetting, desk-top printing, jet setting,
adventure camps, disabled ramps,
homes free of damp, bedside lamps.
Windsurfing, skateboards, roller blades, sailboards,
electric wheelchairs and teddy bears.
These are a few of the things that should go in that box
before fastening it with chains and securing it with locks!

Janis Priestley

My Photo Album 1990-1996

Snapshots may capture one single moment in time
but looking at them now
these images bleed animated real life
as every door is opened
and the stories flow in detail once again.

Dad falling into the pond head first
while trying to rescue Rex the cat from the tree.

Sister's dayglo orange perm gone wrong,
brother's green mohican and nose ring,
mum and dad's embarrassment at
our posh cousin's wedding.

The day we won the cup
and mum got told off by the police
for dancing on the pitch.

The school trip to Scafell Pike where on the group photo
everyone smiles and pulls tongues
except boring Mr Goodwood who doesn't like children
and Wrighty . . . who later got done for mooning.

Posing with my first guitar,
all sunglasses, sneer and spots
on front of my Oasis and U2 posters,
not knowing the guitar was upside down.

And that one, the small one,
all blurred and squashed from the booth at Woolies.
That's me and Sally, my first real girlfriend,
smiling and eating Curly Wurlies.
(It's a good job that was the last photo of the four,
ten seconds later and the camera would have caught us
in the middle of a slurpy chocolate snog . . .)

Good times.
Good times indeed . . .

Paul Cookson

Thinking About The future

When I am old, and the world is very old,
Will there be puddles?
– Puddles that reflect the sky
Puddles for us to splash through
Emptying them out, muddying them?

     I expect so.

Will there be ice cream and treats?
Will there be parties and combing my hair and putting
                  best clothes on
Will there be birthdays and presents and shopping for
                  presents?
And who will be there?

     That I don't know. I don't know.
     But I hope so.

Will there be houses and gardens and toys in a cupboard
And babies to look after and doctors for when you're ill?
Will there be holidays and games on the beach and uncles
                  and aunts?
And food and 'fridges to fill?

     It may be so.

Will there be stories and books and people who can read
                                   what you're writing?
When I am old will there be children who ask me to read
And tell them stories to stop me being cross when they
                                   squabble?
        Well, if you learn to read and write and
                                   teach your children
        Let us hope so.

Will there be an end to time and a great huge fire
That burns all the streets and the houses and we fall
                                   into a pit?
And shall I be burnt and there be nothing to eat
And no animals or pets or school, or water and
                                   parents even?

        That I don't know, I don't know,
        But before it happens
        Shall we go out now while we can
        And play in the snow?

continued

If there are people there in the future, grown-ups and
                                    children,
Will they have boots for the snow? Will they be allowed
To stay up late? What will they do?
And what will they be thinking?

        I don't know what will happen, but if there are
                                people at all
        You can be fairly certain that they'll be worrying
        About the future, and wondering about the past.

Will they be thinking about me?

        Maybe. What do you want for tea?

Jenny Joseph

A Riddle for the Year 2000

My 1st is in many, but never in day,
My 2nd's in visit, but never in stay,
My 3rd is in little and also in lot,
My 4th is in holly, but not within hot.
My 5th is in chicken and also in egg,
My 6th is in pen, but never in peg.
My 7th is in now and also in then,
My 8th is in pencil, but never in pen.
My 9th is in future, but never in years.
My 10th is in mine, but not his or hers.
My whole is a milestone for woman and man,
It measures, indeed, a significant span.

Celia Warren

Unseen

Present met Past,
Said: *I am your Future.*
But Past walked by
Without look or gesture.

Present then strained
To define Past's nature,
But his sight was too short
To catch every feature.

While Present looked back
Absorbed in the creature,
Future walked by;
Unseen; without gesture.

Gerda Mayer